IF FOUND

- _____

✉ _____
   _____

☐ _____

Greater Than a Tourist Book Series
Reviews from Readers

I think the series is wonderful and beneficial for tourists to get information before visiting the city.

-Seckin Zumbul, Izmir Turkey

I am a world traveler who has read many trip guides but this one really made a difference for me. I would call it a heartfelt creation of a local guide expert instead of just a guide.

-Susy, Isla Holbox, Mexico

New to the area like me, this is a must have!

-Joe, Bloomington, USA

This is a good series that gets down to it when looking for things to do at your destination without having to read a novel for just a few ideas.

-Rachel, Monterey, USA

Good information to have to plan my trip to this destination.
-Pennie Farrell, Mexico

Great ideas for a port day.
-Mary Martin USA

Aptly titled, you won't just be a tourist after reading this book. You'll be greater than a tourist!
-Alan Warner, Grand Rapids, USA

Even though I only have three days to spend in San Miguel in an upcoming visit, I will use the author's suggestions to guide some of my time there. An easy read - with chapters named to guide me in directions I want to go.
-Robert Catapano, USA

Great insights from a local perspective! Useful information and a very good value!
-Sarah, USA

This series provides an in-depth experience through the eyes of a local. Reading these series will help you to travel the city with confidence and it'll make your journey a unique one.
-Andrew Teoh, Ipoh, Malaysia

GREATER THAN A TOURIST- ST. CROIX US VIRGIN ISLANDS USA

50 Travel Tips from a Local

Tracy Birdsall

Cover designed by: Ivana Stamenkovic
Cover Image: Tracy Birdsall
Editor: Amanda Wills

CZYK Publishing Since 2011.

Greater Than a Tourist
Visit our website at www.GreaterThanaTourist.com

Lock Haven, PA
All rights reserved.
ISBN: 9781791572365

>TOURIST

50 TRAVEL TIPS FROM A LOCAL

BOOK DESCRIPTION

Are you excited about planning your next trip?

Do you want to try something new?

Would you like some guidance from a local?

If you answered yes to any of these questions, then this Greater Than a Tourist book is for you.

Greater Than a Tourist- St. Croix, US Virgin Islands, United States by Tracy Birdsall offers the inside scoop on St. Croix. Most travel books tell you how to travel like a tourist. Although there is nothing wrong with that, as part of the Greater Than a Tourist series, this book will give you travel tips from someone who has lived at your next travel destination.

In these pages, you will discover advice that will help you throughout your stay. This book will not tell you exact addresses or store hours, but instead, will give you excitement and knowledge from a local that you may not find in other smaller print travel books.

Travel like a local. Slow down, stay in one place, and get to know the people and the culture. By the time you finish this book, you will be eager and prepared to travel to your next destination.

TABLE OF CONTENTS

15. Cruzan Rum since 1760
16. Get Your Workout In
17. Movies and Bowling Exist
18. Jewelry Shopping Joy
19. Plantations and History
20. Famous "Crucians" – The Pride of the Island
21. Farmers Markets Galore
22. Holidays Specific to St. Croix
23. Jump-Up and Moko-Jumbies
24. More Events to Attend – There's Always a Party
25. Buck Island Tours & Sailing Tours
26. Horseback Riding in Paradise
27. Where it's Breezy, A/C not required
28. Point Udall To See it All
29. Beer Drinking Pigs, Oink!
30. Leatherback Brewery – People Drinking Beer, Chug!
31. Bioluminescent Kayaking
32. Flora and Fauna of the Tropics
33. No Open Container Laws
34. Chaney, Chaney, Chaney!
35. Sunset Sailing Tours
36. Snorkeling is Fun & Free
37. Scuba Diving Dreams – The Wall is a Hidden Gem
38. 100 Years of Ice Cream
39. Tan Tan Tours Through the Rainforest

Travel Bucket List
NOTES

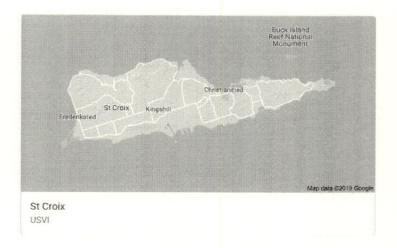

St Croix
USVI

St Croix Climate

	High	Low
January	82	71
February	82	71
March	82	71
April	83	73
May	84	75
June	86	77
July	87	77
August	87	77
September	86	76
October	86	75
November	84	73
December	83	72

GreaterThanaTourist.com

Temperatures are in Fahrenheit degrees.
Source: NOAA

DEDICATION

This book is dedicated to the amazing people of St. Croix and the greater citizens of the US Virgin Islands. The most affectionate and resilient people that have inspired me to adapt and taught me to be resourceful after Hurricanes' Irma and Maria, which devastated the islands in 2017.

And to my two wonderful sons, Wesley and Ian. Wesley's wit, creativity and love has seen us all through the toughest of times. Ian's courage, charm and easy-going attitude brings peace to our family. I love you both tremendously and I am proud to be your mom. To my sons I quote *"Oh, the places you'll go!"* – Dr. Seuss

ABOUT THE AUTHOR

I moved to St. Croix in the US Virgin Islands from Northern California. I am passionate about mentoring and giving back to the community. I spent the last twenty-five years in corporate America and recently decided to live the island life for now. I am enjoying my best life in the Caribbean doing remote consulting and freelancing. I have an MBA in International Management from the Monterey Institute of International Studies and speak multiple languages including fluent Spanish, having lived in Venezuela growing up. I caught the travel bug at a young age. I want to share my passion for life with others. I have always been curious and adventurous. Utopia for me is inspiring others to pursue their dreams. YOLO, you only live once and it's time to do, not just talk about doing!

Most recently I was the Vice President, Head of Specialized Sales North America for VISA Inc. Prior to VISA, I severed as Senior Director of Sales for Equinix, a data center and infrastructure company. Previously, I spent eleven years in the IBM ecosystem. I headed the IBM software group as the executive leader overseeing the entire western US covering all of IBM software.

I am particularly proud of coaching high-tech talent and teams. It gives me the greatest feeling of pride and accomplishment when sales executives achieve their goals and are substantially rewarded with President's clubs and promotions. I love growing leaders and am proud to state that many team members under my direction have grown to be some of the strongest and well-equipped sales leaders in Silicon Valley.

During my free time I enjoy CrossFit, traveling, hanging out at the beach, sailing, scuba diving, snorkeling, reading, cooking, going out on the town and baking. I love spending free time with my teenage sons, family and friends on the island of St. Croix.

The natural beaches and turquoise blue waters are exceptional. The palm trees are captivating. But the greatest delight of the island is captured within the local people and communities. I love St. Croix and whether I am here forever or just a season in life, St. Croix will always have a special place in my heart.

HOW TO USE THIS BOOK

The Greater Than a Tourist book series was written by someone who has lived in an area for over three months. The goal of this book is to help travelers either dream or experience different locations by providing opinions from a local. The author has made suggestions based on their own experiences. Please do your own research before traveling to the area in case the suggested places are unavailable.

Travel Advisories: As a first step in planning any trip abroad, check the Travel Advisories for your intended destination.
https://travel.state.gov/content/travel/en/traveladvisories/traveladvisories.html

FROM THE PUBLISHER

Traveling can be one of the most important parts of a person's life. The anticipation and memories that you have are some of the best. As a publisher of the Greater Than a Tourist book series, as well as the popular 50 Things to Know book series, we strive to help you learn about new places, spark your imagination, and inspire you. Wherever you are and whatever you do I wish you safe, fun, and inspiring travel.

Lisa Rusczyk Ed. D.
CZYK Publishing

OUR STORY

Traveling is a passion of the "Greater Than a Tourist" series creator. Lisa studied abroad in college, and for their honeymoon Lisa and her husband toured Europe. During her travels to Malta, an older man tried to give her some advice based on his own experience living on the island since he was a young boy. She was not sure if she should talk to the stranger but was interested in his advice. When traveling to some places she was wary to talk to locals because she was afraid that they weren't being genuine. Through her travels, Lisa learned how much locals had to share with tourists. Lisa created the "Greater Than a Tourist" book series to help connect people with locals. A topic that locals are very passionate about sharing.

WELCOME TO
> TOURIST

"Jobs fill your pockets, but adventures fill your soul."

- Jaime Lyn Beatty

1. US CITIZENS – PASSPORTS NOT REQUIRED

The USVI is a perfect getaway for everyone. The best aspect for US citizens is that you do not even need a passport to visit. St. Croix, St. John and St. Thomas are United States Territories. Pack a bag and come visit us! You don't need much, as the weather is always nice. There are many direct flights to the island from Miami, Atlanta, Ft. Lauderdale, Puerto Rico, and St. Thomas. We look forward to your visit to the island to enjoy a taste of the colorful and joyful Caribbean culture (aka: "kulcha" in Crucian).

2. ST. CROIX PEOPLE ARE "CRUCIANS"

People from the Virgin Islands are Virgin Islanders, however, based on the island you will also have another nickname. People from St. Croix are called Crucians.

If you are from St. Thomas, you are also known as a St. Thomian. The locals on St. John are called St. Johnians. After only a few weeks' vacation or even 2-years on the island, sadly you would not be considered Crucian, Thomian or Johnian. Typically, only those who have been on the island for decades or those natively born on the island are referred to as Crucians, Thomians or St. Johnians. That said, you are guaranteed to be a Crucian at heart. Crucian can also refer to the creole language spoken by locals on the island of St. Croix.

3. LIFE IN THE LEFT LANE

The left lane is the safe lane. It is believed that we drive on the left side of the road because of St. Croix's historic heritage from the Dutch. Back in the horse and buggy days we drove on the left and have never since tried to change it. Drivers are courteous and a honk of the horn usually means thank you for letting me go ahead of you. If someone flashes their lights at you, it means they are giving you the right of way. So, feel free to honk back (quick double tap) and express your gratitude! Drive safely and always remember to stay on the left side of the road. It is said that on the mainland they drive on the right side of the road and Virgin Islanders drive on the correct side.

4. RENTAL CARS NEEDED FOR EXPLORING

In high season, November through June, it may be difficult to find a rental car on the island of St. Croix. During high season it would be best to reserve a car prior to your arrival. For insurance reasons anyone under 25 is prohibited from renting a car on St. Croix. I highly recommend renting a car to explore the island. St. Croix is the largest of the three US Virgin Islands with eighty-four square miles to explore. It is almost twenty-seven miles from east to west and just about seven miles from the north-shore to the south-shore. Here is a list of car rental places on island:

Centerline Car Rentals 1-888-288-8755 / 340-778-0441

Olympic Rent-a-Car 1-888-USVI-CARS / 340-718-3000

Judi of Croix 1-877-903-2123 / 340-773-2123

Budget Rent-a-Car 1-888-264-8894 / 340-778-9636

Hertz Rent-a-Car 1-888-248-4261 / 340-778-1402

Avis Rent-a-Car 340-713-1347

5. Gas Needed and Tire Patches, Maybe!

The roads are not very well maintained and you will definitely experience a pothole or two while driving on the island. The potholes develop because of the constant tropical rains that leave our island lush, green and beautiful. Due to ongoing construction, you may also experience a nail in your tire. Unfortunately, this is a common experience for us islanders. Ah, yes, island life! Some great places to get a tire patch include: Echo Valley Tires, H&H Tire & Battery, Emerald Tires or Cruzan Tires. As for gas, you will usually pay first inside and then, pump it yourself.

6. Taxis A Plenty

Taxis on St. Croix are usually white vans, not yellow cars with a black stripe or checkers as you may be familiar with on the mainland. There are many taxis on the island. Fares are fixed by law and most are posted, but it is always best to agree on a fare before you go. The popular stops are hotels or the taxi stands located on King Street in Christiansted and Strand Street in Frederiksted. Again, taxi rates are posted. If you have a nice driver and a good fare, it is courteous to tip your driver a couple of dollars. The taxi services on the island are Antilles Taxi, Cruzan Taxi & Tours, St. Croix Taxi and our friend Francis 340-332-9074.

7. ALWAYS GREET (GOOD MORNING, GOOD AFTERNOON, AND GOOD NIGHT)

Crucian hospitality is what makes this island special. The people of St. Croix always greet each other when passing on the streets or in our local grocery stores, post offices, markets, etc. Be sure to greet and reply back with a simple, "good morning", "good afternoon" or "good night" in the evening. Good night is much more common than good evening. Even a simple "good day" will put smile on people's faces and they may even think you are a local. If you are going to ask someone for directions or a recommendation, be sure to start off with a Crucian standard, "good morning", or you might just be ignored and considered rude. The island sometimes takes an adjustment, to get into the slower pace of life. Occasionally we only need to slow down a moment to simply say "good afternoon" and chat with a passerby. This is what makes island time and island life so delightful.

8. LOAD UP ON GROCERIES

There are plenty of grocers on the island of St. Croix and you can actually find almost anything you need or want. The big box grocers are: Plaza Extra East, Plaza Extra West and Pueblo. I would say that Pueblo is on the lower end of the spectrum. I typically shop at Plaza Extra West for my weekly supplies.

Seaside Market is a high-end grocery store where you can pick out fine wines and select from an exceptional cheese assortment. Seaside Market has a great deli where they also sell smoothies and frappes. Quality Foods has an abundant variety of healthy foods, fresh fruits and vegetables. Food Town is good for a quick stop to pick up a few items. If you need to buy in bulk, similar to a Costco or Sam's Club on the mainland, visit Cost-U-Less.

9. CHEAP LOCAL EATERIES

You will see many locals grabbing a plate to go for lunch. It is typical here for a plate to consist of seasoned rice, beans, a small salad and a protein. Standard plates at local eateries range from $11 to $14 dollars at lunch.

I highly recommend the iconic, La Reine Chicken Shack, the best rotisserie chicken on the island of St. Croix (cash only). Their Johnny cakes are also fantastic. In downtown Christiansted, visit Zeny's, the owners are from the Dominican Republic and cook up a fantastic shrimp plate. Kim's downtown Christiansted is also a local favorite. Rosie's has the best mofongo south of Puerto Rico. And if you are just in the mood for a slice of excellent pizza, Napoleon's Pizza is the place to go. Turtle's Deli or Beach Side Café in Frederiksted are nice cheap eateries on the west end. The food trucks on the island are also wonderful, try Killer Tacos or Ana's Living Food truck. Singh's downtown Christiansted is a great place to grab a local boneless curry chicken roti.

10. Local Foods – What is That?

Johnny Cakes – Deep fried dough, an island donut, which is not sweet, however super tasty! It is usually served as a side dish or snack. I think the best ones are at La Reine Chicken Shack.

Pate – Fried snack similar to an empanada, they are usually stuffed with vegetables or meats such as beef, chicken, saltfish, or conch.

Saltfish – Salted cod fish is a staple of the Virgin Islands. Try it on crackers or in a pate.

Kallaloo or Callaloo – A popular Crucian dish where the main ingredient is a green leafy vegetable, usually amaranth or dasheen leaves. Typically cooked with pork or seafood; the seafood is the best.

Fungi – I thought this had something to do with mushrooms, surprisingly it does not. Fungi is a cornmeal dish, like polenta. It is served sometimes in kallaloo. The consistency is like stiff mashed potatoes.

Roti – Indian flat bread, potato, chicken, beef, goat, or other fillings wrapped like a burrito in a roti flatbread.

Rum Cake – Of course you probably already know what rum cake is, however I had to put it on the list because it is truly a local delicacy.

Other local foods include the fruit. Definitely try soursop or non-alcoholic ginger-beer juice. Sorrel is a Christmas drink, but can be found year around, made from sorrel blossoms and hibiscus, yum! Try tamarind juice if you love sweet and tart or a coquito if you prefer alcohol around the holidays.

11. FANCIER MEALS FOR THE EPICUREAN

Culinary has truly found its place on the island of St. Croix. For a nice relaxing epicurean meal do consider the following: Galangal; Asian Thai fusion. These four top restaurants; Savant, Balter, 17□/64□, and Zion Modern Kitchen all offer a great ambiance and an excellent menu selection of gourmet eclectic choices to please even the most pretentious of tastes. The Bombay Club is more mid-range and also offers a unique ambiance and varietal menu.

12. RESTAURANTS ON MY ROTATION LIST

Rum Runners at Hotel Caravelle – nice view on the boardwalk and variety selection

Christine's – hidden and nestled away, excellent lunch

Duggan's – great seafood

Cheeseburgers in Paradise – quick bite, great for families / groups

Blue Water Terrace – excellent seafood and large portions

40 Strand – on our monthly rotation and an excellent choice

The Mill Boardwalk Bar & Brick Oven Pizza - casual

Shupes on the Boardwalk – casual, burgers/fries, bar

Toast – breakfast arepas

Café Fresco – outdoor coffee, breakfast and brunch eatery

Tap Deck Bar & Billiards – bar food and nightly music

Braata – local renowned chef, Digby Stridion, West Indian cuisine

No Bones Café – mid-west style eatery

Un Amore – best Italian on the island

Maria's Cantina – best Mexican on the island (except for Killer Tacos, which is a food truck)

Rowdy Joes – Northshore eatery near Cane Bay

Flyers – Northshore eatery at Salt River

Uptown Eatery – fresh salads and healthy eats

BES Cocktail – for cocktails from the best mixologist on St. Croix

No judgement, sometimes traveling with kids they just want the franchises. St. Croix also has KFC, Dominos, McDonalds, Wendy's, Subway and a former IHOP now known as CHOP.

13. BEACHES FOR DAYS

St. Croix is known for warm Caribbean waters and turquoise blue seas. As a cultural tidbit, beach clothes (bathing suits) are for the beach only. It is against custom and culture to walk the streets in your bikini. That said, it is more than ok at the beach bars and beaches!

Rainbow Beach – excellent beach with Rhythms restaurant and West End Water Sports

Sandy Pointe National Wildlife Refuge – to see the sea turtles

Shoys Beach – quiet neighborhood beach

Cane Bay Beach – beautiful locals beach with restaurants nearby, great for snorkeling and diving

Half Penny Beach – located on the south shore

Mermaid Beach at Buccaneer – beach at the hotel and restaurant, rent water sports equipment, kayaks, SUPs, chairs, etc.

Pelican Cove, Sugar Beach & Gentle Winds - waterfront condos providing great beach fronts for guests and visitors

Salt River Beach – see night Bioluminescent Kayaking (there is also a small beach some locals visit in Salt River)

14. Beach Bar Bests

Here is a quick listing of the best beach bars on the island. Grab a seat, have an island drink or a quick bite to eat and relax. Rhythms at Rainbow Beach, Louis and Nachos on the west end, Chenay Bay on the east end, Mermaid Beach at The Buccaneer, Eat at Cane Bay, The Deep End Bar & Grill at Green Cay Marina, Carambola Resort, and Sand Castles Beach Side Café in Frederiksted.

15. Cruzan Rum since 1760

The ultimate pride and joy of the island is Cruzan rum. The distillery has been managed by the Nelthropp family for over eight generations. The distillery has been on the sugar mill property and in operation for over 250 years. Crucians love their 5 to 12-year aged rums and the many varieties of flavored rums. My favorite flavored rum is guava; however, my best friends prefer coconut, banana and passion fruit. The tour is an absolute must see and you may even run into a Nelthropp. As a bonus, you will get to taste the molasses and have two complimentary rum drinks at the factory. You can put the lime in the coconut and shake it all up, as long as you don't forget to add the

Cruzan rum! Local tip, you can usually find Cruzan rum cheaper at a grocery store or Cost-U-Less than at the distillery itself. Rum drinks are very popular on island with the best ones being the painkiller, the bushwhacker, and a dark and stormy with ginger-beer.

16. GET YOUR WORKOUT IN

I personally love CrossFit! Come visit me at 340CrossFit in Christiansted. Drop-ins are always welcomed and invited to become part of the family. Spin, spin and more spin. There are two places I know of that offer spin classes daily: Ride into Fitness (where you can also grab an awesome fresh fruit açaí bowl) and iCycle which offers spin classes in a newer, fresh vibe experience.

Beeston Hill Gym is a great gym for those who prefer a lot of equipment and working out on their own circuit or training schedule. Studio 360 offers a variety of classes such as boxing, yoga and personal training.

Yoga is offered at many places including The Courtyard in Christiansted and SUP Yoga at Chenay Bay, where you can also get a massage.

St. Croix has an annual Triathlon called Beauty & The Beast which was historically the Ironman 70.3. The tradition continues in America's paradise. There is a long course, as well as a sprint where participants can enter individually or as a relay. See you there!

17. MOVIES AND BOWLING EXIST

Although we are only an island of fifty thousand, we do have a lot of facilities for fun! My sons love going to our newly remodeled Caribbean Cinema's movie theatre in Sunny Isle. This theater is so amazing that you can order beer or wine, chill and watch the show. There are multiple screens and they play the latest releases. Movies are usually released a day earlier on St. Croix than on the mainland.

The bowling facility, Tropical Ten Pins, isn't as new and remodeled, however, it is a great place to check out for a fun night of bowling, especially when it's raining outside. The facility has a bar, restaurant and lounge.

18. JEWELRY SHOPPING JOY

Handcrafted goods are the best treasures and gifts. Bonus: on the island of St. Croix there is no sales tax. The Virgin Islands is known for its famous hook bracelet and uniquely designed necklace pendants and rings. These special items on St. Croix can be found at many places, I recommend:

Crucian Gold, known for their famous crucian knot bracelet. Since early 1970, the Bishop family has owned and operated Crucian Gold. Icon Brian Bishop perfected his skills as a jeweler by tying sailing knots with precious metal wire. I highly recommend Crucian Gold.

IB Design with Whealan Massicott, trained by Mr. Bishop, is a newcomer to the jewelry scene and has definitely made his mark with his unique handcrafted island designs and reputation for the finest of gold and silver.

Sonya's makes a unique custom bracelet for every hurricane. The latest design of course is the Irma and the Maria hurricane bracelet. Sonya's is also known for the more traditional St. Croix hook bracelet.

Joyia, another local artist and her husband, hand craft with a personal touch and surf designs.

I will warn you that other jewelers on the island may tell you their designs are originals; however, they are likely exact duplicates and knock offs from the shops mentioned above. Other shops also produce their jewelry off island, usually in the Dominican Republic. Therefore, to ensure you are truly taking home a St. Croix original souvenir, made on the island of St. Croix, I would suggest sticking to the shops mentioned above. Thank you for supporting our local businesses.

19. PLANTATIONS AND HISTORY

An unfortunate history of slavery exists on the island. However, we must keep the history alive to understand the impact so that it never occurs again. There are many gracious guides to tell us stories of the past and the reality of plantation life. Below are some of the landmark plantations on the island of St. Croix.

Whim Plantation Museum is a twelve-acre landmark, featuring restored ruins, a cook house, tropical trees and a small sugarcane field. The stately authentically furnished Greathouse welcomes guests as you walk around the historic 18th century buildings of the former sugar plantation estate.

Lawaetz Family Museum is operated by the St. Croix Landmarks Society. This is a traditional homestead museum. The Danish West Indian home has lush gardens and orchards and authentic furnishings. The home was in the Lawaetz family for over one hundred years.

20. FAMOUS "CRUCIANS" – THE PRIDE OF THE ISLAND

Tim Duncan, former NBA superstar, is proudly from the island of St. Croix. Tim was a professional NBA basketball player, known for his time with the San Antonio Spurs. Tim is a five-time NBA Champion and three-time MVP, most valuable player. Tim Duncan only started playing basketball in ninth grade, after Hurricane Hugo destroyed the island of St. Croix. Tim was a fantastic swimmer, until Hurricane Hugo destroyed the only Olympic sized swimming pool on St. Croix, located at Good Hope Country Day School. Once the pool was destroyed, Tim's coach suggested he take up another sport. He became a basketball legend, and the rest is history. Tim Duncan does not forget his roots and always remembers the people of the island of St. Croix. He is an active philanthropist on the island.

Tim generously donated to the island of St. Croix after the devastating hurricanes in 2017.

21. FARMERS MARKETS GALORE

Supporting local farmers and eating healthy go hand in hand. Sejah Farms is open daily from 10am to 5pm. I love their naturally spicy arugula lettuce. Art Farm is a treat and only open on Wednesday afternoons and Saturday mornings. The best papaya I have ever tasted in my life came from Art Farm. Lawaetz Museum in Frederiksted hosts a farmer's market on Wednesday and Saturday mornings as well. Ridge to Reef is an eco-tourist camp. Ridge to Reef does not sell produce on the farm, however they do have farm to table events to attend and their produce can be found at Lawaetz farmers' market previously mentioned.

La Reine Farmer's market is the largest on St. Croix on Saturday and Wednesday mornings. A myriad of large and small farmers and local vendors come to sell everything from locally caught seafood and fish, to plants, honey and toasted plantain chips. I love going to La Reine farmers market early on Saturday mornings.

22. HOLIDAYS SPECIFIC TO ST. CROIX

Carnival / J'ouvert is a week-long period of partying and pageantry. This leads up to the parade featuring colorful costumes and dancing downtown on the streets. Unique floats and pounding drum beats of the steel bands boost the islands' spirit. Each of the islands has its own Carnival, St. Croix's season starts during Crucian Christmas Festival in mid-December. There are four unofficial holidays during this celebratory time: Food Fair, J'ouvert, the Children's Parade and finally the Adult Parade. The Adult Parade is usually held on the Saturday closest to January 6th, Epiphany Day, which is also known as Three Kings Day. All of these events run at the same time as the main event in Festival Village, Frederiksted. The fairgrounds have live nightly music entertainment as well as many local food vendors, rides, drinks and games for all ages. Below are the dates of holidays' specific to the island:

Jan. 1 Crucian Children's Festival

Jan. 2 Crucian Adult Festival and Parade

Jan. 6 Three Kings Day / Epiphany Day

March 31 Transfer Day VI from Denmark

July 3 Emancipation Day, VI (Abolition of Slavery Danish West Indies)

47

Oct 12 Columbus Day (aka: USVI & Puerto Rico Friendship Day)

Nov. 1 D. Hamilton Jackson Day (aka: Bread & Bull Day)

23. JUMP-UP AND MOKO-JUMBIES

Jump Up is held four times a year (6pm – 10pm) and is a city-wide street party in downtown Christiansted. Come on down and enjoy the dancing celebration. Music (including steel pan ensembles), local food, drinks, street vendors, cultural dancers, shopping, live bands, fire dancers, as well as the traditional Moko Jumbies all come together. It is a great event for everyone, including families.

February – on the Friday closest to Valentine's Day

May – on the first Friday of May

July – on the Friday closest to Alexander Hamilton Day

November – on the Friday after Thanksgiving

Moko Jumbies are the famous stilt-walkers and dancers. They are usually dressed in bright colors and sometimes wear carnival masks and head decorations. Moko means healer in Central Africa and jumbie is a spirit or ghost in the West Indies. Moko-Jumbies are

now an official symbol of the US Virgin Islands. If you
see one, take the time to watch, because according to
legend they bring good luck.

24. MORE EVENTS TO ATTEND –
THERE'S ALWAYS A PARTY

Taste of St. Croix happens annually. Restaurants,
chefs, farmers, distributors, fisherman, caterers and
distillers all meet up, while attendees go from booth to
booth sampling all the delicacies being presented. Live
music and entertainment as well as wine, beer and
spirits flow.

St. Croix Food & Wine Experience is another annual
food event on the island. Forbes magazine voted this
one of the "Ten Best International Food and Wine
Festivals". This event is for foodies and pretentious
epicureans. The wine and food experience takes place
in April. Celebrity chefs, as well as local chefs, cook
and show off their talents.

Agrifest, is the agricultural food fair of the US
Virgin Islands and is a huge three-day event featuring
agriculture and livestock from all over the Caribbean.
Vendors from several islands join together to share

food, music and fun. It is also known as AgriFair and takes place in February.

St. Patrick's Day is a wild celebration on the island of St. Croix. Downtown Christiansted has a massive parade and everyone seems to come out for this event. Be sure to wear green because on this day everyone on the island of St. Croix is Irish.

Easter weekend the entire island camps out. People sleep on the beaches in tents and share food with anyone who asks. On Easter weekend it is an island tradition to pitch a tent and go camping.

25. Buck Island Tours & Sailing Tours

Each of the three Virgin Islands has its very own "Buck Island", however, St. Croix's is a historic national monument, underwater national park and preserve. A great place for natural snorkeling, swimming, beautiful turquoise waters, sandy beaches and good hiking, you will see many charter boats and also locals on the weekends. The park is over 176 acres above and under water and is proclaimed to be "one of the finest marine gardens in the Caribbean Sea." There is no fee to access the island, however, the only access is via boat. Private boats offer full-day and half-day excursions by booking with one of many tour operators. The most recognized are:

Big Beard's Adventure Tours 1-866-773-4482 / 340-773-4482

Buck Island Charters 340-718-3161

Caribbean Sea Adventures 340-773-2628

Jolly Roger 340-513-2508

26. Horseback Riding in Paradise

My youngest son truly enjoys the beach horseback riding in the water and on the sand at Cane Bay. He just loved his adventure with Cowboy Steve. You can book a horseback ride with Cowboy Steve at Equus Rides in St. Croix. Steve has gentle horses and provides horses and rides for all skill levels and ages. It was so much fun to watch my son galloping. Steve made sure we got in a lot of photo opportunities and the beach ride was truly amazing. Cruzan Cowgirls and Paul & Jill's Equestrian Stables also provide horseback riding adventures on the island, however, I have not personally been on their tours.

27. WHERE IT'S BREEZY, A/C NOT REQUIRED

The winds and breezes come from the East. The eastern winds typically provide a consistent wind from this direction throughout the year, which is great for sailing and predicting the weather. There is a saying on the island about the "Christmas winds", as it seems the windiest on the island in December. If you rent a place during your visit, just ask if it faces East and then you know that a/c is not required. Otherwise, in the hottest humid months, July through early October, it may be wise to rent a location with air conditioning.

28. POINT UDALL TO SEE IT ALL

The easternmost point of the United States. From Point Udall on the east end of St. Croix, you can go no further. Take a drive and bring a camera to take pictures of the huge life-size sundial and views, views, and more views as far as the eye can see. The sundial is a Millennial Memorial and was put in place for New Years to celebrate the year 2000.

29. BEER DRINKING PIGS, OINK!

Perhaps you have read about the pigs that love drinking beer. It is true and not a myth! Mt. Pellier in the heart of St. Croix's rainforest and jungle is the place to go to feed the pigs a beer. Today the bar is only allowed to serve the pigs near beer, so purchase an O'Doul's at the bar and head on back to feed the pigs awaiting their favorite beverage. The pigs will literally crush the entire can right in front of you and beg for more.

30. LEATHERBACK BREWERY – PEOPLE DRINKING BEER, CHUG!

Prior to 2017, there was no beer on tap on the island of St. Croix. Bottles or cans were the only way to enjoy a cold beer on the island. We are so thrilled to have Leatherback Brewery who now supplies all three Virgin Islands with draft beer from a tap. Excellent beer brewed fresh right here on the island. The brewery has many events throughout the year so be sure to take a look at their calendar online. To accompany the beer, you can also grab some small bites and appetizers as you enjoy the company of many locals who stop in for a pint. We thank you for supporting local businesses.

31. BIOLUMINESCENT KAYAKING

Salt River Bay National Historic Park and Ecological Preserve is managed by the National Park Service and VI government. Kayaking at night is a spectacular adventure and a once in a lifetime opportunity to see the natural bioluminescent bay at Salt River on the island of St. Croix. Guided kayak tours featuring bioluminescence, glow in the dark microorganisms, can be seen at the Salt River and Altona Lagoon. The ecological tours are breathtaking. I recommend the following tour operators:

See Thru Kayaks VI, tours in clear bottom kayaks

Virgin Kayak Tours, history buff, highly informative tours

Bush Tribe Eco Adventures, canoe, kayak and other off the beaten path local adventures

32. FLORA AND FAUNA OF THE TROPICS

St. George Village Botanical Garden features lush gardens, tropical rainforest and restored village buildings. The gardens are open daily, except

Christmas. The botanical collection boasts over 1500 native and exotic species and varieties. The Garden is also the site of the annual "Mango Melee", an annual celebration of mangos, typically held in July.

When we arrived on the island of St. Croix, my children enrolled in a bush camp to learn about all the magnificent flora and fauna on the island. We learned about which plans are poisonous, hallucinogenic, and which ones are healing, like the tan-tan bush and the aloe plants. The island is full of unique reptiles, iguanas, and small deer. The bush is beautiful and the island possess many magnificent mahogany trees lining our roads. Keep an eye out for the Virgin Islands territory bird, the bananaquit, scientific name, Coereba flaveola, or to us Virgin Islanders, the pretty yellow breasted bird.

33. No Open Container Laws

Yes, you can have an open beer, wine or rum bottle in your car while driving, but driving under the influence is prohibited. St. Croix does not tolerate drunk driving. Since there are no laws restricting open containers, this also means that you can freely walk around downtown or the boardwalk sipping your favorite spirit of choice.

34. CHANEY, CHANEY, CHANEY!

Chaney is a small piece of smooth porcelain that can be found on the beaches and on plantations. No one is sure how the small beautiful fragments of chaney appeared, but many believe it is from ship passengers throwing porcelain overboard to avoid tax during the slave rebellion in 1878. Chaney is beautiful and many have great blue designs of old plates and porcelain antiquities. Local craftsmen have started turning chaney into wonderful pieces of jewelry. This is a highly unique piece you can take from St. Croix as a souvenir. Chaney Chicks is a fantastic store on the boardwalk in Christiansted to purchase wonderful hand-crafted and rare pieces of chaney jewelry. Say hello to the shop owner, Denise, for me. Crucian Gold and other jewelers on the island also handcraft remarkable and unique chaney treasures.

35. SUNSET SAILING TOURS

Sunsets on the water are gorgeous and they never get old. Most of the sailing charters mentioned under Buck Island Tours also do sunset sails. I suggest making a reservation as the sunset sails do book up in season with both locals and tourists alike.

Lyric Sails offers excellent live music aboard their sunset cruise. It is a very lively and romantic setting with a cash bar and food catered by local restaurants. Some of the sunset cruises are inclusive of appetizers and free rum punch. If you are fortunate, you will see dolphins and flying fish as you sail into the sunset. The sail back is an amazing stargazing experience.

The Roseway is a historic ninety-year-old wooden sailboat. The Roseway Sunset Sail operates only during high season, typically November through March. When the Roseway is not in St. Croix, it's home-base is Boston, MA. It is an active National Historic Landmark owned by the World Ocean School. The Roseway has been completely restored to its original magnificent beauty. Create a very unique opportunity by booking a ride on a historic sailing ship and enjoy the stunning sunset off the island of St. Croix.

36. Snorkeling is Fun & Free

There are many snorkeling locations just off the beach shores. Simply rent or purchase snorkeling gear on the island at our local Kmart or the many dive and swim shops around St. Croix. You can swim out to the wall at Cane Bay and snorkel to your heart's content. Closer to shore look into snorkeling at Rainbow Beach (head towards the right of the buoys), Isaac Bay, The Palms or under the pier in Frederiksted. Davis Bay and Tamarind Reef are two local favorites. Several boats are also available to take you out for a day or half-day of snorkeling. Those include the ones listed under Buck Island Tours. Buck Island is a whimsical snorkeling opportunity. Other sailing charters mentioned are Caribbean Sea Adventures, Big Beard and Jolly Rogers. Several of the dive shops cited below can also provide snorkeling day trips.

37. Scuba Diving Dreams – The Wall is a Hidden Gem

St. Croix, hands down, has the best diving in all of the Virgin Islands. The underwater geography is breathtaking. There are over fifty dive sites to choose from and most with untouched and unseen coral, sponges, schools of tropical fish, sea turtles and moray eels. The luckiest divers get a chance to swim with the dolphins that hang out in the waters of St. Croix.

Butler Bay has shallow and deep wreck dives which consist of three shipwrecks, along an old NOAA hydro lab. All of the wrecks have amazing colorful coral and schools of reef fish swimming around.

Cane Bay Dive Shop

Sweet Bottom Dive Shop

N2 Blue Waters

Dive Experience

The Frederiksted pier is also a great place for beginners to dive or snorkel, just jump off the pier. This is a shallow dive which makes it great for novice divers and you will most certainly see some colorful schools of fish. If it is your lucky day, you may even spot a seahorse.

38. 100 Years of Ice Cream

Wow! Wow! Armstrong's Ice Cream has literally been serving up ice cream on St. Croix for over 100 years. Armstrong's is located on the west end in Frederiksted on the Christiansted Bypass. You will definitely want to try some of the local fruit flavors like tamarind, sour sop or gooseberry. Armstrong also has the traditional flavors such as vanilla, cookies and cream, chocolate and banana. The weather is always nice enough to stop in for ice cream.

39. Tan Tan Tours Through the Rainforest

Jeep through the jungle mud or take a 2-mile hike to the Annaly Bay Tide Pools. The tide pools can be dangerous during high tide so be sure to go with a guide. If you bring your snorkeling gear you can see crabs, sea urchins and schools of fish.

Book a jeep adventure with little hiking with Tan Tan Tours on St. Croix. Numerous visitors claim the Tan Tan tour was the highlight of their visit to St. Croix. The tour operator has several tours, including a full-day, half-day, tide pool visits or simply a scenic and beach run tour. The jeeps take you on a breathtaking journey through the rainforest and up the mountains for views unseen by most visiting or even living on St. Croix.

40. HERMIT CRAB RACES

For a fun afternoon or evening and a chance at winning some great prizes and adventures on St. Croix, go to the hermit crab races. You can bring your own hermit crab you found on the beach that day or pick one of the crabs for the five-gallon bucket. The smaller crabs actually move faster than one would expect. You also get to name your crab and root for the winner to cross the finish line. Tito and Sue host the races three times a week. The races are a great deal of fun for all ages to enjoy. See the St. Croix calendar online for locations and times.

41. CAPTAIN MORGAN'S SPICES IT UP

Captain Morgan Distillery tours are also available at their distillery located along the Melvin Evans Highway. St. Croix's rum industry continues to rise. In 2008, Diageo and the US Virgin Islands began an initiative for the construction and operation of this high capacity rum distillery. Captain Morgan's famous spiced rum is made on St. Croix. The tour is available with souvenir gift shop onsite.

42. THE REFINERY IS OUR LIVELIHOOD

Although tourism is the main sources of revenue on St. Croix. Another top economic revenue source is Saint Croix's oil refinery. In the high times, St. Croix was home to Hovensa one of the world's largest oil refineries. Unfortunately, Hovensa closed down in 2012 and over 2,000 St. Croix residents lost their jobs. Most recently, in 2018, the refinery has started to reopen due to new investors and with the assistance of the USVI government. The refinery is now called Limetree Bay Terminals and is currently a storage facility for oil, with plans to refine again. This has brought a better economy to the island and created new jobs for the people of St. Croix. Many visitors may see the refinery as an eye sore on the island. The locals see it as sustaining our livelihood.

43. MORE DINING – BBQ & CUBANO SANDWICHES

Blues Backyard BBQ & Grill is a great place to have a drink and a brisket or pulled pork sandwich. Have a seat at the bar and chat with the local regulars that frequent Blues. Blues has live entertainment weekly so be sure to take a look at their calendar for the line-up.

Nauti Bar & Grill is a newcomer to the island with excellent barbequed meats and seafood. Nauti's is a great place to play some darts or a round of billiards while enjoying some excellent BBQ.

Smoke STX on the west end in Frederiksted knows how to smoke up some fantastic meats.

Ziggy's Island Market has barbeque on most days of the week and is also known for their Cubano sandwiches.

Quality Grocers Deli, not to be confused with Quality Foods (a grocery store), has the most amazing Cubano sandwiches on the island. Quality Grocers Deli is located in Estate La Grande Princesse. Be sure to order it spicy for an extra kick.

44. Slang, Sayings and Nuances

"Dem" is used to make any noun plural. Mongoose "dem" is the plural for mongoose, not mongeese or mongooses but mongoose "dem". The cat "dem" means two or more cats. "Heh" means here. "Meeno" is to say, I don't know. "Fortrue" is the equivalent to, really? "Whe pah u deh?" is to ask where are you?

Asking for directions may be difficult because we don't really know street names on St. Croix. A typical direction might be, it's the fourth palm tree on the left or take a right after the blue fence. Landmarks such as mango trees, palm trees, or someone's cousin's house may be all the directions you get and we are sincere when giving.

"Sweet eye" is a flirty glance at someone while a "cut eye" is a disdainful look. "Aiight" is slang for alright and is more common than ok or fine. "Baan ya" means the person was born here and is a native. "Cheese and bread" is slang to express frustration or disapproval and is a rude way of saying it, similar to OMG.

Some other quick definitions for you; a "gongolo" is a millipede and they are everywhere, "faddah" and "muddah" are father and mother, "limin" is hanging out and relaxing, "soon come" means coming soon, "ting" means thing. "Nyampe" is mucus in the corner of your eye. Twin City, like the Twin City Coffee House, refers to the two towns of Christiansted and Frederiksted on the island of St. Croix.

45. THE WEATHER IS SO NICE

Virgin Island weather is so nice, musical artist, Pressure, made a song about it called "Virgin Islands Nice". The song has become a theme song for most islanders. The weather all year around fluxuates between 82 to 89 degrees Fahrenheit. Rainy and hurricane season is considered low season, late June through the end of October. High tourist season begins mid-October and lasts through early June.

46. VEGAN FOOD SUSTAINS NUMEROUS

Agriculture on the island of St. Croix is fantastic! Vegans and vegetarians eat like kings and queens. There is a high population of vegans and vegetarians on the island of St. Croix. Some island vegan eateries include;

Ital in Paradise – this is my favorite and chef Chris knows how to cook up the lentil balls. Vegan Heaven is also fantastic and located near Gallows Bay. Keep an eye out for the Healthy Living Food Truck, where vegan and vegetarian plates are cooked up daily.

47. HISTORIC FIGURES & NOTABLE RESIDENTS OF ST. CROIX

Salt River is also known as Christopher Columbus Landing. Columbus landed at this spot in America's paradise in 1493. Legend has it that Columbus encountered the not-so-friendly Carib Indian tribe. This led to the first documented conflict between Europeans and Native Americans. Some believe that Columbus never set foot on land. Instead it is believed he sent out a search party from his ship to explore the new land.

Alexander Hamilton, born in Nevis, was a famous resident of St. Croix. Alexander Hamilton was an American statesman and the first United States Secretary of the Treasury. Most recently, there is an award-winning "Hamilton" Broadway musical, selling out to audiences everywhere. Hamilton is known for the Constitutional Convention and was a major author of the Federalist papers. Hamilton's St. Croix history started in 1745 when his mother first visited the island. It is known that Hamilton lived on the island of St. Croix from 1765-1772 (at the age of 8-15) and there are various sites on the island to learn more about his history.

48. Jet Skis, Sport Fishing & Land Lovers Bike Tour

West End Water Sports at Rainbow beach is the best place to rent jet skis, stand up paddle boards or fly boards; a jetpack propelled by water. You can also rent snorkel gear at West End Water Sports or a beach chair and umbrella to simply relax and enjoy the sun and sand. The beach at Green Cay Marina, The Buccaneer Resort, and Chenay Bay, allow you to rent kayaks, stand up paddle boards and beach chairs as well.

Sport fishing is allowed from shore and no license is required. If you prefer to charter, there are many sport fishing charters on the island. A few of them are Hook and Sun Fishing Charters, Fishing St. Croix Forever and Always Charters, Blue Canyon Charters and Captain Cook Charters.

For land lovers, there is a bike tour operator on the island to take you on a beautiful bicycle tour of the lush island. Virgin Islands Bike and Trails aka: VI Bike and Trails, formerly known as Freedom City Cycles.

49. Mailing Gone Postal

When I first moved to St. Croix, I found shipping on and off island to be difficult. It turns out that it is not at all. Since we are a US Territory there are six US Post Offices on the island. It is easy to mail a postcard home, to share your trip with relatives and friends. In today's internet age, it is probably quicker to post an Instagram picture or a Facebook post. I personally feel a postcard adds a genuine and authentic touch to say, "wishing you were here". For larger shipments to and from St. Croix, you can use: Paradise Freight or VI Cargo.

50. CASINOS TO GAMBLE – WIN OR LOSE

St. Croix has two open casinos on the island to hopefully allow you to strike it big! The island also has plans to develop an additional casino in the coming years. The Caravelle Casino has a variety of slot machines and a service bar. It is located at the Caravelle Hotel in downtown Christiansted. Divi Carina Bay Resort & Casino located on the east end of the island is the largest casino, with slot machines and table games. There are plans in place for the development of a casino on the South shore to be named either St. Croix Golf Resort and Casino or Seven Hills Golf Resort and Casino. Good luck!

BONUS TIP 1. BINGO WITH THE LOCALS

Bingo is big on the island of St. Croix, with some jackpots reaching over $1,000 USD. Bingo rotates from different restaurants around the island and habitually takes place twice a week. Tuesday night is regularly at Off the Wall Restaurants near Cane Bay. The fun starts at 6pm so come early, buy your bingo cards and settle in with your rum drink of choice. You can always check the St. Croix Calendar for the exact location and weekly time.

BONUS TIP 2. LEATHERBACK TURTLES AT SANDY POINT

Sandy Point was designated a Natural National Landmark in 1980 and is located on St. Croix's west end. The U.S. Fish and Wildlife Department manages the beachfront. Sandy Point is the largest leatherback turtle nesting site in the U. S. Sandy Point is only open on Saturdays and Sundays (holidays included), and when a cruise ship is in port. There is no admission to enter the park. Sandy Point is the most beautiful sand strip and the longest stretch of beach in the U.S. Virgin

Islands. Depending on when the turtles begin their nesting season, Sandy Point is closed from about mid-May until the beginning of September so the turtles can nest untouched in their natural habitat. You can watch the sea turtles lay eggs, one of the most fascinating sights to see. If you are fortunate enough, you can also see the turtles hatching.

BONUS TIP 3. HISTORICAL LANDMARKS – THE TWIN CITY FORTS

Fort Christiansted, currently serves as headquarters for the National Park Service and is a great historical fort. The colorful and bright yellow fort overlooks Christiansted Harbor and Protestant Cay. The fort has several colonial military architectural buildings including: The Danish Customs House, the Scale house, Government House, Danish West India & Guinea Company Warehouse and the Steeple Building, all which date back to the earliest period, 18th century. The fort is open to the public seven days a week except Thanksgiving and Christmas.

Fort Frederik is located left of the cruise ship pier as you disembark in Frederiksted. This fort was built in the mid-1700's and remains in use for the military and other governmental purposes. The fort is typically open Monday through Friday and closed holidays.

BONUS TIP 4. WALKING AREAS

St. Croix has two main charming towns, known as the Twin City, Christiansted and Frederiksted. Christiansted has a beautiful boardwalk with restaurants and shops, the wharf area is now designated as a National Historic Site by the National Park Service. The town of Christiansted has narrow streets and old Danish style architecture.

Frederiksted is where most of the large cruise ships dock. Frederiksted is known as "freedom city". The Frederiksted pier has a lovely waterfront and several blocks of shops and restaurants. The town features an Old Customs House, the Fleming Building, constructed of bricks from destroyed sugar mills.

Bonus Tip 5. Coffee Shops and Books

No small town or island would be complete without its local coffee shops and bookstore. The best coffee shops to sit and enjoy the local atmosphere are: Twin City Coffee House; located in downtown Christiansted, Polly's on the Pier; located in Frederiksted, and The Bistro Coffee & Eatery; located at Gallows Bay. Café Fresco with outdoor seating in downtown Christiansted is a wonderful place for coffee and an excellent breakfast. Undercover Books is a fantastic little bookstore, located next door to The Bistro Coffee & Eatery at Gallows Bay.

Bonus Tip 6. Golf the Greenest Greens

The beauty of the tropical island truly shines through on the greenest golfing greens in the world. St. Croix has two wonderful 18-hole golf courses for the golf lovers that visit.

Carambola Golf and Tennis Club is just east of the rainforest. This is an outstanding course designed by Robert Trent Jones. The course hosts a popular tournament, an annual LPGA Tournament in the

Spring. The facilities include a pro shop with equipment rentals and a restaurant, plus an after-golf bar overlooking the course.

The Buccaneer Hotel has an 18-hole challenging course. Many say the uphill third hole overlooking the ocean offers the greatest of challenges and not to mention, breathtaking vista.

The Reef offers a 9-hole challenging golf experience for guests and the general public. This is a great spot for pros and new golfers alike.

BONUS TIP 7. STUFF YOU NEED & WHERE TO GET IT

Sunscreen, bug spray, more souvenirs, towels, shampoo and miscellaneous things you forgot to bring on your trip to St. Croix can be found. Do not fear or have anxiety because you can literally find 99.999% of what you need on the island. It may not be as accessible or convenient, but we do have it. The island has a few shopping malls, although nothing like the mainland, Gallows Bay, Sunny Isle and Sunshine Mall. One of the least expensive places to buy St. Croix key chains, t-shirts and tank tops is at Kmart. There are two Kmart's on the island, as well as a Kmart Appliance store. Home Depot is a big box retailer on the island and is a great place to pick up some mosquito repellant. For a higher end souvenir shop, I recommend the Purple Papaya in downtown Christiansted near the boardwalk.

BONUS TIP 8. MUSIC FOR THE SOUL

St. Croix is known internationally for the St. Croix Jazz and Caribbean Music and Art Festival that takes place every spring. This event draws world renowned jazz artists to perform on the island. The music scene on St. Croix is very vibrant. Restaurants, beaches and bars feature live music almost daily. Everything from pop, reggae, jazz and piano can be heard loudly resonating across the island. The cultural Caribbean genres of music include calypso, salsa, and soca, as well as reggae originating from Jamaica. I was so excited when my youngest son decided to learn how to play the steel pans. Where else in the world can you learn to be a pannist! Pannist use these unique metal drums that some say look like the bottom of an old steel garbage bin.

Riddims is St. Croix's top music and culture shop located in downtown Christiansted. This retail shop has the latest in reggae, hip-hop, soca, calypso, steel pan, quelbe, reggaeton and more. If you are looking to bring home the sounds of the Caribbean, head on over to Riddims for unique musical souvenirs.

BONUS TIP 9. POWER, MOBILE & WIFI

You may hear locals complain about WAPA. WAPA is the Water and Power Authority providing the islands' electricity and water. Unfortunately, part of island life is experiencing power outages. Most restaurants, hotels and other local business are equipped with backup generators. After hurricanes Maria and Irma, most homes also have a small backup generators that can at least continue to run a refrigerator. As a local, we experience a power outage about once a month. The power is usually back up within thirty minutes, so do not fear, the power will be back quick.

Mobile cell phone reception covers approximately eighty-five to ninety percent of the island. There are definitely dead zones. Standing next to a tall palm tree does really help with reception. AT&T provides the best coverage, although Sprint and others work similarly well.

Wifi is exceptional on the island of St. Croix. Three of the internet's largest submarine cables connect here; the Pan America Crossing Cable, the South American Crossing cable and the MAC (Mid-Atlantic Crossing Cable). The island literally sits on top of more Internet bandwidth than the city of New York. This makes St. Croix a paradise for remote high-tech workers like myself.

Bonus Tip 10. Healthcare & Emergencies

While I hope you will not need to read this section, it is important to know about the healthcare and emergency facilities on the island of St. Croix. We have two hospitals on the island; Governor Juan Luis Hospital and the Charles Harwood Memorial Hospital. The Juan Luis Hospital Emergency room is open 24/7. Air ambulances are available for medivac situations. Airplanes are typically chartered to either Miami or Puerto Rico.

For walk-in clinic needs, I recommend Plessen Healthcare or Frederiksted Healthcare. The island also has the Caribbean Kidney Center and many excellent specialized physicians, pediatricians, optometrists, dermatologist, dentists and more.

TOP REASONS TO BOOK THIS TRIP

Beaches: The beaches here are the best and the weather is always nice.

The Good-natured People: Friendly locals await your visit and we always have an excuse for a party.

Something for Everyone: Water Sports, Hiking, Restaurants and Shopping

Rum: Cruzan Rum and Captain Morgan's Spiced Rum Distilleries

Assortment of Natural Beauty: Flora, Fauna & Picturesque Vistas

Bragging Rights: Relaxing in America's Paradise gets you swagger

Island Culture: A rich heritage of tradition and local foods

OTHER RESOURCES:

http://www.stcroixcalendar.com

https://www.visitusvi.com

https://www.visitstcroix.com

https://www.travelandleisure.com/travel-guide/us-virgin-islands

https://virginislandsthisweek.com/st-croix/

https://www.stxenvironmental.org

http://stcroixlandmarks.com

https://www.gotostcroix.com

http://www.stcroixtourism.com

https://www.nhc.noaa.gov

BONUS BOOK

50 THINGS TO KNOW ABOUT PACKING LIGHT FOR TRAVEL

PACK THE RIGHT WAY EVERY TIME

AUTHOR: MANIDIPA BHATTACHARYYA

Edited by Melanie Howthorne

ABOUT THE AUTHOR

Manidipa Bhattacharyya is a creative writer and editor, with an education in English literature and Linguistics. After working in the IT industry for seven long years she decided to call it quits and follow her heart instead. Manidipa has been ghost writing, editing, proof reading and doing secondary research services for many story tellers and article writers for about three years. She stays in Kolkata, India with her husband and a busy two year old. In her own time Manidipa enjoys travelling, photography and writing flash fiction.

Manidipa believes in travelling light and never carries anything that she couldn't haul herself on a trip. However, travelling with her child changed the scenario. She seemed to carry the entire world with her for the baby on the first two trips. But good sense prevailed and she is again working her way to becoming a light traveler, this time with a kid.

INTRODUCTION

He who would travel happily must travel light.

-Antoine de Saint-Exupéry

Travel takes you to different places from seas and mountains to deserts and much more. In your travels you get to interact with different people and their cultures. You will, however, enjoy the sights and interact positively with these new people even more, if you are travelling light.

When you travel light your mind can be free from worry about your belongings. You do not have to spend precious vacation time waiting for your luggage to arrive after a long flight. There is be no chance of your bags going missing and the best part is that you need not pay a fee for checked baggage.

People who have mastered this art of packing light will root for you to take only one carry-on, wherever you go. However, many people can find it really hard to pack light. More so if you are travelling with children. Differentiating between "must have" and "just in case" items is the starting point. There will be ample shopping avenues at your destination which are just waiting to be explored.

This book will show you 'packing' in a new 'light' – pun intended – and help you to embrace light packing practices for all of your future travels.

Off to packing!

DEDICATION

I dedicate this book to all the travel buffs that I know, who have given me great insights into the contents of their backpacks.

THE RIGHT TRAVEL GEAR

1. CHOOSE YOUR TRAVEL GEAR CAREFULLY

While selecting your travel gear, pick items that are light weight, durable and most importantly, easy to carry. There are cases with wheels so you can drag them along – these are usually on the heavy side because of the trolley. Alternatively a backpack that you can carry comfortably on your back, or even a duffel bag that you can carry easily by hand or sling across your body are also great options. Whatever you choose, one thing to keep in mind is that the luggage itself should not weigh a ton, this will give you the flexibility to bring along one extra pair of shoes if you so desire.

2. CARRY THE MINIMUM NUMBER OF BAGS

Selecting light weight luggage is not everything. You need to restrict the number of bags you carry as well. One carry-on size bag is ideal for light travel. Most carriers allow one cabin baggage plus one purse, handbag or camera bag as long as it slides under the seat in front. So technically, you can carry two items of luggage without checking them in.

3. PACK ONE EXTRA BAG

Always pack one extra empty bag along with your essential items. This could be a very light weight duffel bag or even a sturdy tote bag which takes up minimal space. In the event that you end up buying a lot of souvenirs, you already have a handy bag to stuff all that into and do not have to spend time hunting for an appropriate bag.

I'm very strict with my packing and have everything in its right place. I never change a rule. I hardly use anything in the hotel room. I wheel my own wardrobe in and that's it.

Charlie Watts

87

Clothes & Accessories

4. Plan Ahead

Figure out in advance what you plan to do on your trip. That will help you to pick that one dress you need for the occasion. If you are going to attend a wedding then you have to carry formal wear. If not, you can ditch the gown for something lighter that will be comfortable during long walks or on the beach.

5. Wear That Jacket

Remember that wearing items will not add extra luggage for your air travel. So wear that bulky jacket that you plan to carry for your trip. This saves space and can also help keep you warm during the chilly flight.

6. Mix and Match

Carry clothes that can be interchangeably used to reinvent your look. Find one top that goes well with a couple of pairs of pants or skirts. Use tops, shirts and jackets wisely along with other accessories like a scarf or a stole to create a new look.

7. CHOOSE YOUR FABRIC WISELY

Stuffing clothes in cramped bags definitely takes its toll which results in wrinkles. It is best to carry wrinkle free, synthetic clothes or merino tops. This will eliminate the need for that small iron you usually bring along.

8. DITCH CLOTHES PACK UNDERWEAR

Pack more underwear and socks. These are the things that will give you a fresh feel even if you do not get a chance to wear fresh clothes. Moreover these are easy to wash and can be dried inside the hotel room itself.

9. CHOOSE DARK OVER LIGHT

While picking your clothes choose dark coloured ones. They are easy to colour coordinate and can last longer before needing a wash. Accidental food spills and dirt from the road are less visible on darker clothes.

10. WEAR YOUR JEANS

Take only one pair of Jeans with you, which you should wear on the flight. Remember to pick a pair that can be worn for sightseeing trips and is equally eloquent for dinner. You can add variety by adding light weight cargoes and chinos.

11. Carry Smart Accessories

The right accessory can give you a fresh look even with the same old dress. An intelligent neck-piece, a couple of bright scarves, stoles or a sarong can be used in a number of ways to add variety to your clothing. These light weight beauties can double up as a nursing cover, a light blanket, beach wear, a modesty cover for visiting places of worship, and also makes for an enthralling game of peek-a-boo.

12. Learn To Fold Your Garments

Seasoned travellers all swear by rolling their clothes for compact and wrinkle free packing. Bundle packing, where you roll the clothes around a central object as if tying it up, is also a popular method of compact and wrinkle free packing. Stacking folded clothes one on top of another is a big no-no as it makes creases extreme and they are difficult to get rid of without ironing.

13. Wash Your Dirty Laundry

One of the ways to avoid carrying loads of clothes is to wash the clothes you carry. At some places you might get to use the laundry services or a Laundromat but if you are in a pinch, best solution is to wash them yourself. If that is the plan then carrying quick drying clothes is highly recommended, which most often also happen to be the wrinkle free variety.

14. Leave Those Towels Behind

Regular towels take up a lot of space, are heavy and take ages to dry out. If you are staying at hotels they will provide you with towels anyway. If you are travelling to a remote place, where the availability of towels look doubtful, carry a light weight travel towel of viscose material to do the job.

15. Use A Compression Bag

Compression bags are getting lots of recommendation now days from regular travellers. These are useful for saving space in your luggage when you have to pack bulky dresses. While packing for the return trip, get help from the hotel staff to arrange a vacuum cleaner.

Footwear

16. Put On Your Hiking Boots

If you have plans to go hiking or trekking during your trip, you will need those bulky hiking boots. The best way to carry them is to wear them on flight to save space and luggage weight. You can remove the boots once inside and be comfortable in your socks.

17. Picking The Right Shoes

Shoes are often the bulkiest items, along with being the dainty if you are a female. They need care and take up a lot of space in your luggage. It is advisable therefore to pick shoes very carefully. If you plan to do a lot of walking and site seeing, then wearing a pair of comfortable walking shoes are a must. For more formal occasions you can carry durable, light weight flats which will not take up much space.

18. Stuff Shoes

If you happen to pack a pair of shoes, ensure you utilize their hollow insides. Tuck small items like rolled up socks or belts to save space. They will also be easy to find.

TOILETRIES

19. STASHING TOILETRIES

Carry only absolute necessities. Airline rules dictate
that for one carry-on bag, liquids and gels must be in
3.4 ounce (100ml) bottles or less, and must be packed
in a one quart zip-lock bag. If you are planning to stay
in a hotel, the basic things will be provided for you. It's
best is to buy the rest from the local market at your
destination.

20. TAKE ALONG TAMPONS

Tampons are a hard to find item in a lot of countries.
Figure out how many you need and pack accordingly.
For longer stays you can buy them online and have
them delivered to where you are staying.

21. GET PAMPERED BEFORE YOU TRAVEL

Some avid travellers suggest getting a pedicure and
manicure just the day before travelling. This not only
gives you a well kept look, you also save the trouble of
packing nail polish. Remember, every little bit of
weight reduced adds up.

Electronics

22. Lugging Along Electronics

Electronics have a large role to play in our lives today. Most of us cannot imagine our lives away from our phones, laptops or tablets. However while travelling, one must consider the amount of weight these electronics add to our luggage. Thankfully smart phones come along with all the essentials tools like a camera, email access, picture editing tools and more. They are smart to the point of eliminating the need to carry multiple gadgets. Choose a smart phone that suits all your requirements and travel with the world in your palms or pocket.

23. Reduce the Number of Chargers

If you do travel with multiple electronic devices, you will have to bear the additional burden of carrying all their chargers too. Check if a single charger can be used for multiple devices. You might also consider investing in a pocket charger. These small devices support multiple devices while keeping you charged on the go.

24. Travel Friendly Apps

Along with smart phones come numerous apps, which are immensely helpful in our travels. You name it and you have an app for it at hand – take pictures, sharing with friends and family, torch to light dark roads, maps, checking flight/train times, find hotels and many other things. Use these smart alternatives to traditional items like books to eliminate weight and save space.

I get ideas about what's essential when packing my suitcase.

-Diane von Furstenberg

Travelling With Kids

25. Bring Along the Stroller

Kids might enjoy walking for a while but they soon tire out and a stroller is the just the right thing for them to rest in while you continue your tour. Strollers also double duty as a luggage carrier and shopping bag holder. Remember to pick a light weight, easy to handle brand of stroller. Better yet, find out in advance if you can rent a stroller at your destination.

26. BRING ONLY ENOUGH DIAPERS FOR YOUR TRIP

Diapers take up a lot of space and add to the weight of your luggage. Therefore it is advisable to carry just enough diapers to last through the trip and a few for afterwards, till you buy fresh stock at your destination. Unless of course you are travelling to a really remote area, in which case you have no choice but to carry the load. Otherwise diapers are something you will find pretty easily.

27. TAKE ONLY A COUPLE OF TOYS

Children are easily attracted by new things in their environment. While travelling they will find numerous 'new' objects to scrutinize and play with. Packing just one favorite toy is enough, or if there is no favorite toy leave out all of them in favor of stories or imaginary games.

28. CARRY KID FRIENDLY SNACKS

Create a small snack counter in your bag to store away quick bites for those sudden hunger pangs. Depending on the child's age this could include chocolates, raisins, dry fruits, granola bars or biscuits. Also keep a bottle of water handy for your little one. These things do not add much weight and can be adjusted in a handbag or knapsack.

29. GAMES TO CARRY

Create some travel specific, imaginary games if you have slightly grown up children, like spot the attractions. Keep a coloring book and colors handy for in-flight or hotel time. Apps on your smart phone can keep the children engaged with cartoons and story books. Older children are often entertained by games available on phones or tablets. This cuts the weight of luggage down while keeping the kids entertained.

30. LET THE KIDS CARRY THEIR LOAD

A good thing is to start early sharing of responsibilities. Let your child pick a bag of his or her choice and pack it themselves. Keep tabs on what they are stuffing in their bags by asking if they will be using that item on the trip. It could start out being just an entertainment bag initially but with growing years they will learn to sort the useful from the superfluous. Children as little as four can maneuver a small trolley suitcase like a pro- their experience in pull along toys credit. If you are worried that you may be pulling it for them, you may want to start with a backpack.

31. Decide on Location for Children to Sleep

While on a trip you might not always get a crib at your destination, and carrying one will make life all the more difficult. Instead call ahead to see if there are any cribs or roll out beds for children. You may even put blankets on the floor. Weave them a story about camping and they will gladly sleep without any trouble.

32. Get Baby Products Delivered At Your Destination

If you are absolutely paranoid about not getting your favourite variety of diaper or brand of baby food, check out online stores like amazon.com for services in your destination city. You can buy things online ahead of your travel and get them delivered to your hotel upon arrival.

33. Feeding Needs Of Your Infants

If you are travelling with a breastfed infant, you save the trouble of carrying bottles and bottle sanitization kits. For special food, or medications, you may need to call ahead to make sure you have a refrigerator where you are staying.

34. Feeding Needs of Your Toddler

With the progression from infancy to toddler, their dietary requirements too evolve. You will have to pack some snacks for travelling time. Fresh fruits and vegetables can be purchased at your destination. Most of the cities you travel to in whichever part of the world, will have baby food products and formulas, available at the local drug-store or the supermarket.

35. Picking Clothes for Your Baby

Contrary to popular belief, babies can do without many changes of clothes. At the most pack 2 outfits per day. Pack mix and match type clothes for your little one as well. Pick things which are comfortable to wear and quick to dry.

36. Selecting Shoes for Your Baby

Like outfits, kids can make do with two pairs of comfortable shoes. If you can get some water resistant shoes it will be best. To expedite drying wet shoes, you can stuff newspaper in them then wrap them with newspaper and leave them to dry overnight.

37. KEEP ONE CHANGE OF CLOTHES HANDY

Travelling with kids can be tricky. Keep a change of clothes for the kids and mum handy in your purse or tote bag. This takes a bit of space in your hand luggage but comes extremely handy in case there are any accidents or spills.

38. LEAVE BEHIND BABY ACCESSORIES

Baby accessories like their bed, bath tub, car seat, crib etc. should be left at home. Many hotels provide a crib on request, while car seats can be borrowed from friends or rented. Babies can be given a bath in the hotel sink or even in the adult bath tub with a little bit of water. If you bring a few bath toys, they can be used in the bath, pool, and out of water. They can also be sanitized easily in the sink.

39. CARRY A SMALL LOAD OF PLASTIC BAGS

With children around there are chances of a number of soiled clothes and diapers. These plastic bags help to sort the dirt from the clean inside your big bag. These are very light weight and come in handy to other carry stuff as well at times.

Pack with a Purpose

40. Packing for Business Trips

One neutral-colored suit should suffice. It can be paired with different shirts, ties and accessories for different occasions. One pair of black suit pants could be worn with a matching jacket for the office or with a snazzy top for dinner.

41. Packing for A Cruise

Most cruises have formal dinners, and that formal dress usually takes up a lot of space. However you might find a tuxedo to rent. For women, a short black dress with multiple accessory options will do the trick.

42. Packing for A Long Trip Over Different Climates

The secret packing mantra for travel over multiple climates is layering. Layering traps air around your body creating insulation against the cold. The same light t-shirt that is comfortable in a warmer climate can be the innermost layer in a colder climate.

Reduce Some More Weight

43. Leave Precious Things At Home

Things that you would hate to lose or get damaged leave them at home. Precious jewelry, expensive gadgets or dresses, could be anything. You will not require these on your trip. Leave them at home and spare the load on your mind.

44. Send Souvenirs by Mail

If you have spent all your money on purchasing souvenirs, carrying them back in the same bag that you brought along would be difficult. Either pack everything in another bag and check it in the airport or get everything shipped to your home. Use an international carrier for a secure transit, but this could be more expensive than the checking fees at the airport.

45. Avoid Carrying Books

Books equal to weight. There are many reading apps which you can download on your smart phone or tab. Plus there are gadgets like Kindle and Nook that are thinner and lighter alternatives to your regular book.

CHECK, GET, SET, CHECK AGAIN

46. STRATEGIZE BEFORE PACKING

Create a travel list and prepare all that you think you need to carry along. Keep everything on your bed or floor before packing and then think through once again – do I really need that? Any item that meets this question can be avoided. Remove whatever you don't really need and pack the rest.

47. TEST YOUR LUGGAGE

Once you have fully packed for the trip take a test trip with your luggage. Take your bags and go to town for window shopping for an hour. If you enjoy your hour long trip it is good to go, if not, go home and reduce the load some more. Repeat this test till you hit the right weight.

48. ADD A ROLL OF DUCT TAPE

You might wonder why, when this book has been talking about reducing stuff, we're suddenly asking you to pack something totally unusual. This is because when you have limited supplies, duct tape is immensely helpful for small repairs – a broken bag, leaking zip-lock bag, broken sunglasses, you name it and duct tape can fix it, temporarily.

49. List of Essential Items

Even though the emphasis is on packing light, there are things which have to be carried for any trip. Here is our list of essentials:

• Passport/Visa or any other ID

• Any other paper work that might be required on a trip like permits, hotel reservation confirmations etc.

• Medicines – all your prescription medicines and emergency kit, especially if you are travelling with children

• Medical or vaccination records

• Money in foreign currency if travelling to a different country

• Tickets- Email or Message them to your phone

50. Make the Most of Your Trip

Wherever you are going, whatever you hope to do we encourage you to embrace it whole-heartedly. Take in the scenery, the culture and above all, enjoy your time away from home.

On a long journey even a straw weighs heavy.

-Spanish Proverb

Packing and Planning Tips

A Week before Leaving

- Arrange for someone to take care of pets and water plants.

- Stop mail and newspaper.

- Notify Credit Card companies where you are going.

- Change your thermostat settings.

- Car inspected, oil is changed, and tires have the correct pressure.

- Passports and photo identification is up to date.

- Pay bills.

- Copy important items and download travel Apps.

- Start collecting small bills for tips.

Right Before Leaving

- Clean out refrigerator.

- Empty garbage cans.

- Lock windows.

- Make sure you have the proper identification with you.

- Bring cash for tips.

- Remember travel documents.

- Lock door behind you.

- Remember wallet.

- Unplug items in house and pack chargers.

READ OTHER GREATER THAN A TOURIST BOOKS

Greater Than a Tourist San Miguel de Allende Guanajuato Mexico: 50 Travel Tips from a Local by Tom Peterson

Greater Than a Tourist – Lake George Area New York USA: 50 Travel Tips from a Local by Janine Hirschklau

Greater Than a Tourist – Monterey California United States: 50 Travel Tips from a Local by Katie Begley

Greater Than a Tourist – Chanai Crete Greece: 50 Travel Tips from a Local by Dimitra Papagrigoraki

Greater Than a Tourist – The Garden Route Western Cape Province South Africa: 50 Travel Tips from a Local by Li-Anne McGregor van Aardt

Greater Than a Tourist – Sevilla Andalusia Spain: 50 Travel Tips from a Local by Gabi Gazon

Greater Than a Tourist – Kota Bharu Kelantan Malaysia: 50 Travel Tips from a Local by Aditi Shukla

Children's Book: Charlie the Cavalier Travels the World by Lisa Rusczyk

> TOURIST

Visit Greater Than a Tourist for Free Travel Tips
http://GreaterThanATourist.com

Sign up for the Greater Than a Tourist Newsletter for discount days, new books, and travel information:
http://eepurl.com/cxspyf

Follow us on Facebook for tips, images, and ideas:
https://www.facebook.com/GreaterThanATourist

Follow us on Pinterest for travel tips and ideas:
http://pinterest.com/GreaterThanATourist

Follow us on Instagram for beautiful travel images:
http://Instagram.com/GreaterThanATourist

> TOURIST

Please leave your honest review of this book on Amazon and Goodreads. Please send your feedback to GreaterThanaTourist@gmail.com as we continue to improve the series. We appreciate your positive and constructive feedback. Thank you.

METRIC CONVERSIONS

TEMPERATURE

110° F —   — 40° C
100° F —
90° F —   — 30° C
80° F —
70° F —   — 20° C
60° F —
50° F —   — 10° C
40° F —
32° F —   — 0° C
20° F —
10° F —   — -10° C
0° F —
-10° F —   — -18° C
-20° F —   — -30° C

To convert F to C:

Subtract 32, and then multiply by 5/9 or .5555.

To Convert C to F:

Multiply by 1.8 and then add 32.

32F = 0C

LIQUID VOLUME

To Convert:	Multiply by
U.S. Gallons to Liters	3.8
U.S. Liters to Gallons	26
Imperial Gallons to U.S. Gallons	1.2
Imperial Gallons to Liters	4.55
Liters to Imperial Gallons	22

1 Liter = .26 U.S. Gallon
1 U.S. Gallon = 3.8 Liters

DISTANCE

To convert	Multiply by
Inches to Centimeters	2.54
Centimeters to Inches	39
Feet to Meters	.3
Meters to Feet	3.28
Yards to Meters	91
Meters to Yards	1.09
Miles to Kilometers	1.61
Kilometers to Miles	.62

1 Mile = 1.6 km
1 km = .62 Miles

WEIGHT

1 Ounce = .28 Grams
1 Pound = .4555 Kilograms
1 Gram = .04 Ounce
1 Kilogram = 2.2 Pounds

Travel Questions

- Do you bring presents home to family or friends after a vacation?

- Do you get motion sick?

- Do you have a favorite billboard?

- Do you know what to do if there is a flat tire?

- Do you like a sun roof open?

- Do you like to eat in the car?

- Do you like to wear sunglasses in the car?

- Do you like toppings on your ice cream?

- Do you use public bathrooms?

- Did you bring your cell phone and does it have power?

- Do you have a form of identification with you?

- Have you ever been pulled over by a cop?

- Have you ever given money to a stranger on a road trip?

- Have you ever taken a road trip with animals?

- Have you ever went on a vacation alone?

- Have you ever run out of gas?

- If you could move to any place in the world, where would it be?

- If you could travel anywhere in the world, where would you travel?

- If you could travel in any vehicle, which one would it be?

- If you had three things to wish for from a magic genie, what would they be?

- If you have a driver's license, how many times did it take you to pass the test?

- What are you the most afraid of on vacation?

- What do you want to get away from the most when you are on vacation?

- What foods smells bad to you?

- What item do you bring on ever trip with you away from home?

- What makes you sleepy?

- What song would you love to hear on the radio when you're cruising on the highway?

- What travel job would you want the least?

- What will you miss most while you are away from home?

- What is something you always wanted to try?

- What is the best road side attraction that you ever saw?

- What is the farthest distance you ever biked?

- What is the farthest distance you ever walked?

- What is the weirdest thing you needed to buy while on vacation?

- What is your favorite candy?

- What is your favorite color car?

- What is your favorite family vacation?

- What is your favorite food?

- What is your favorite gas station drink or food?

- What is your favorite license plate design?

- What is your favorite restaurant?

- What is your favorite smell?

- What is your favorite song?

- What is your favorite sound that nature makes?

- What is your favorite thing to bring home from a vacation?

- What is your favorite vacation with friends?

- What is your favorite way to relax?

- Where is the farthest place you ever traveled in a car?

- Where is the farthest place you ever went North, South, East and West?

- Where is your favorite place in the world?

- Who is your favorite singer?

- Who taught you how to drive?

- Who will you miss the most while you are away?

- Who if the first person you will contact when you get to your destination?

- Who brought you on your first vacation?

- Who likes to travel the most in your life?

- Would you rather be hot or cold?

- Would you rather drive above, below, or at the speed limited?

- Would you rather drive on a highway or a back road?

- Would you rather go on a train or a boat?

- Would you rather go to the beach or the woods?

TRAVEL BUCKET LIST

1.

2.

3.

4.

5.

6.

7.

8.

9.

10.

Made in the USA
Middletown, DE
06 November 2019